JET FIGHTERS
Coloring Book

John Batchelor

DOVER PUBLICATIONS, INC.
Mineola, New York

Note

At the end of the Second World War, military aircraft of the world underwent a momentous change. Most World War II airplanes had piston engines and were propeller-driven. The "Jet Revolution" began with the use of the turbine engine, and these jet fighters quickly replaced the old piston-engine planes in air forces after the war. Postwar planes were created for air superiority in speed, power, fuel efficiency, and aerodynamic design. Not only are fighter planes used in combat, but they may also be produced as reconnaissance versions that carry cameras and radar to gain information.

High speed and rate of climb were important features that needed development. Soon, prototype aircraft were breaking records for speed and altitude. A milestone in military combat aircraft design was reached in 1947 when Captain Charles Yeager broke the sound barrier—his plane was traveling at the speed of sound! This is known as *supersonic* speed, or 660 mph at 40,000 feet. During the 1950s, supersonic fighter planes were becoming standard equipment for air forces around the world. Supersonic flight is measured in Mach numbers, an engineering term named after Austrian physicist Dr. Ernst Mach. Mach 1 equals the speed of sound at a given altitude and Mach 2 refers to twice the speed of sound.

Early supersonic planes had limited range and designers set out to improve their features. Technological improvements like internal refueling were perfected in short order. New innovations in military aircraft, as seen in the American Stealth Fighter, were refined. Aircraft design is ever-changing; once production of a plane has commenced, very often plans for a new, improved prototype are already rapidly progressing.

Bibliographical Note

Jet Fighters Coloring Book is a new work, first published by Dover Publications, Inc., in 1998.

International Standard Book Number: 0-486-40357-2

Manufactured in the United States of America
Dover Publications, Inc., 31 East 2nd Street, Mineola, N.Y. 11501

1. **Avro CF-100 (Canada).** A Canadian all-weather two-seater, the Avro CF-100 served the Royal Canadian Air Force. An early prototype was first flown in 1952. The armament of the CF-100 included either eight 0.5-in. machine guns or forty-eight air-to-air rocket missiles. Its fuselage is 54 feet 2 inches long. With a range of about 1,700 miles, the CF-100 could attain a maximum speed at sea level of 660 mph, with a rate of climb of 10,000 feet per minute.

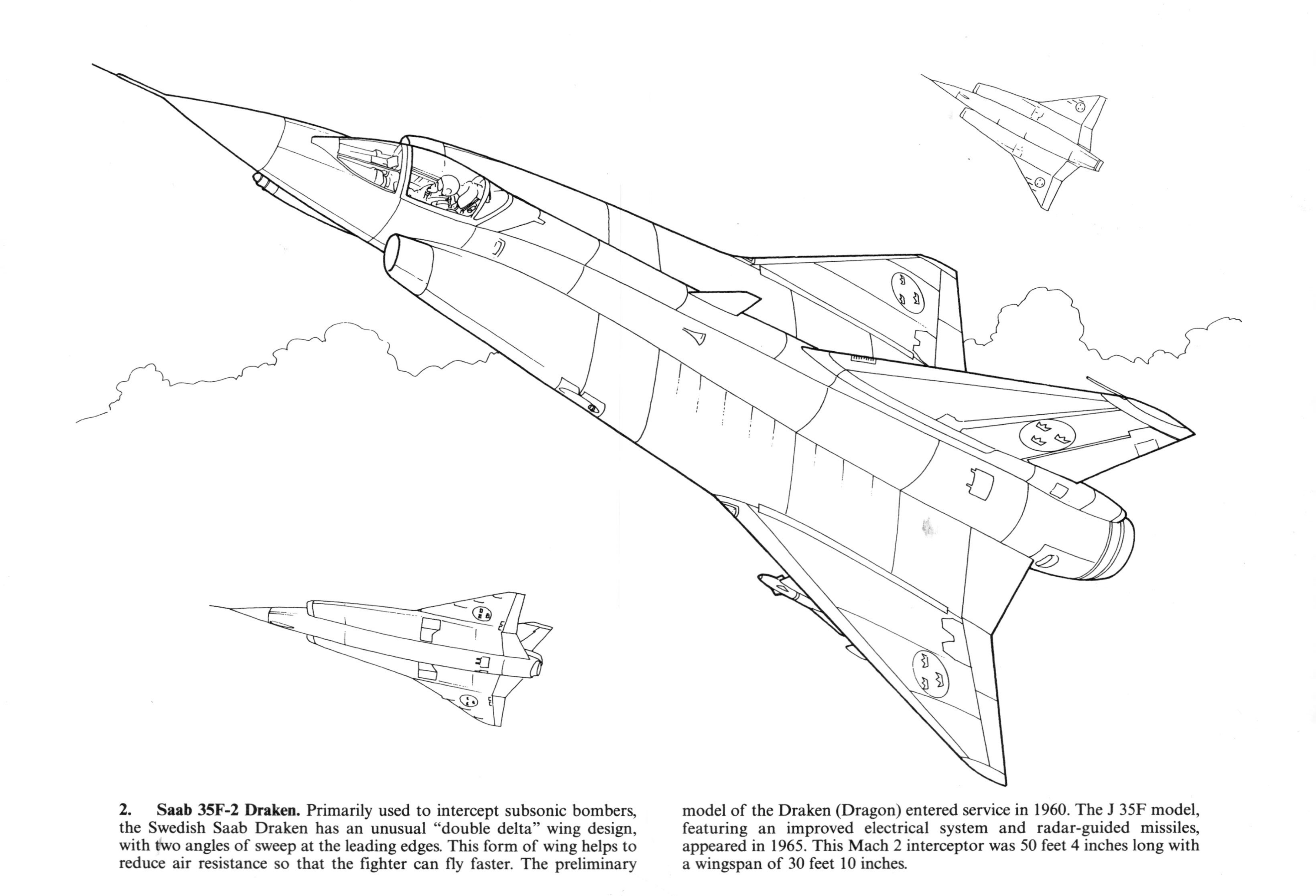

2. Saab 35F-2 Draken. Primarily used to intercept subsonic bombers, the Swedish Saab Draken has an unusual "double delta" wing design, with two angles of sweep at the leading edges. This form of wing helps to reduce air resistance so that the fighter can fly faster. The preliminary model of the Draken (Dragon) entered service in 1960. The J 35F model, featuring an improved electrical system and radar-guided missiles, appeared in 1965. This Mach 2 interceptor was 50 feet 4 inches long with a wingspan of 30 feet 10 inches.

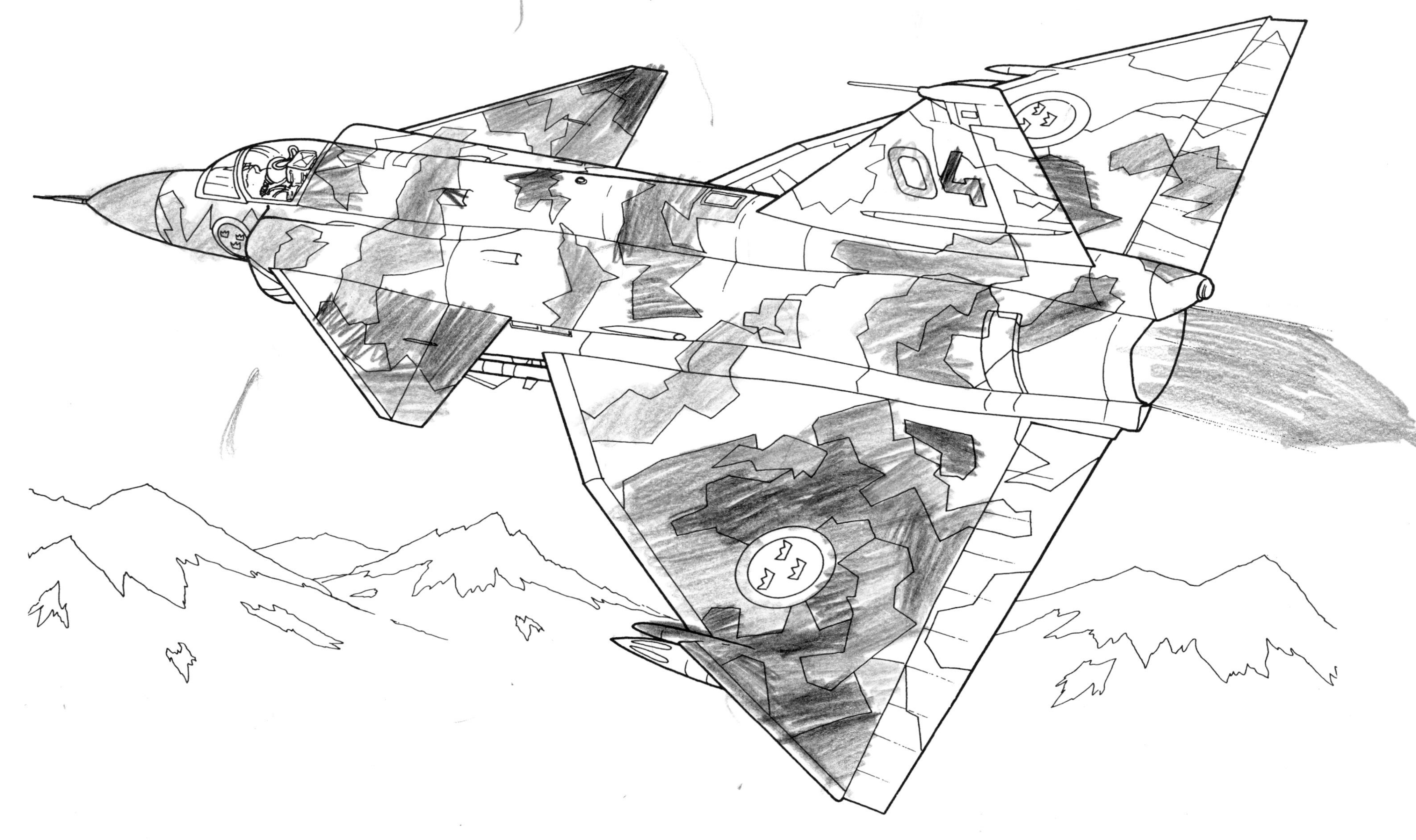

3. Saab JA 37 Viggen. Powered by a Volvo RM 8B turbofan, the JA 37 Viggen (Thunderbolt) was originally designed as a single-seat attack aircraft. With a close-coupled delta configuration, the JA 37's basic airframe was useful for a number of roles. First flown in 1977, the JA 37 was soon re-engineered for use as an interceptor fighter. Production of the Swedish aircraft began in 1979, continuing until 1990. Its maximum speed is 1,365 mph or Mach 2.1. This plane is 53 feet 9¾ inches long and has a wingspan of 34 feet 9¼ inches.

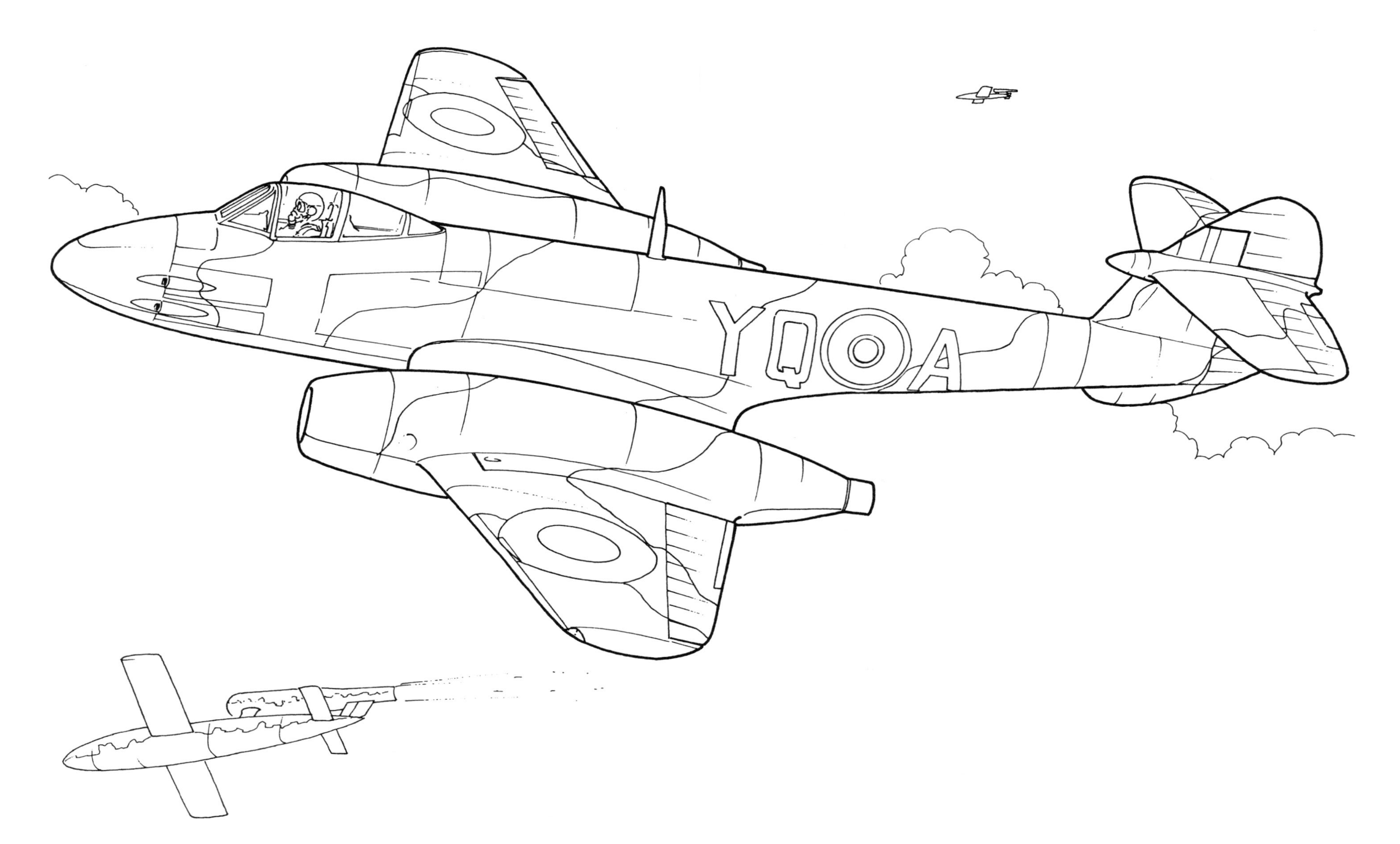

4. Gloster Meteor F Mk 1 616 Sqdn. Produced in 1944, the Gloster Meteor was the first jet fighter to be delivered to a service unit. The British Meteor was supplied to the 616 Squadron. First flown in 1943, the initial model of the Meteor underwent many adjustments due to early problems. It was manufactured in many different versions, including the Meteor II, which had a more powerful engine, and the Meteor III, which had an improved canopy and lower drag. Subsequent versions of the Meteor also had a larger fuel capacity.

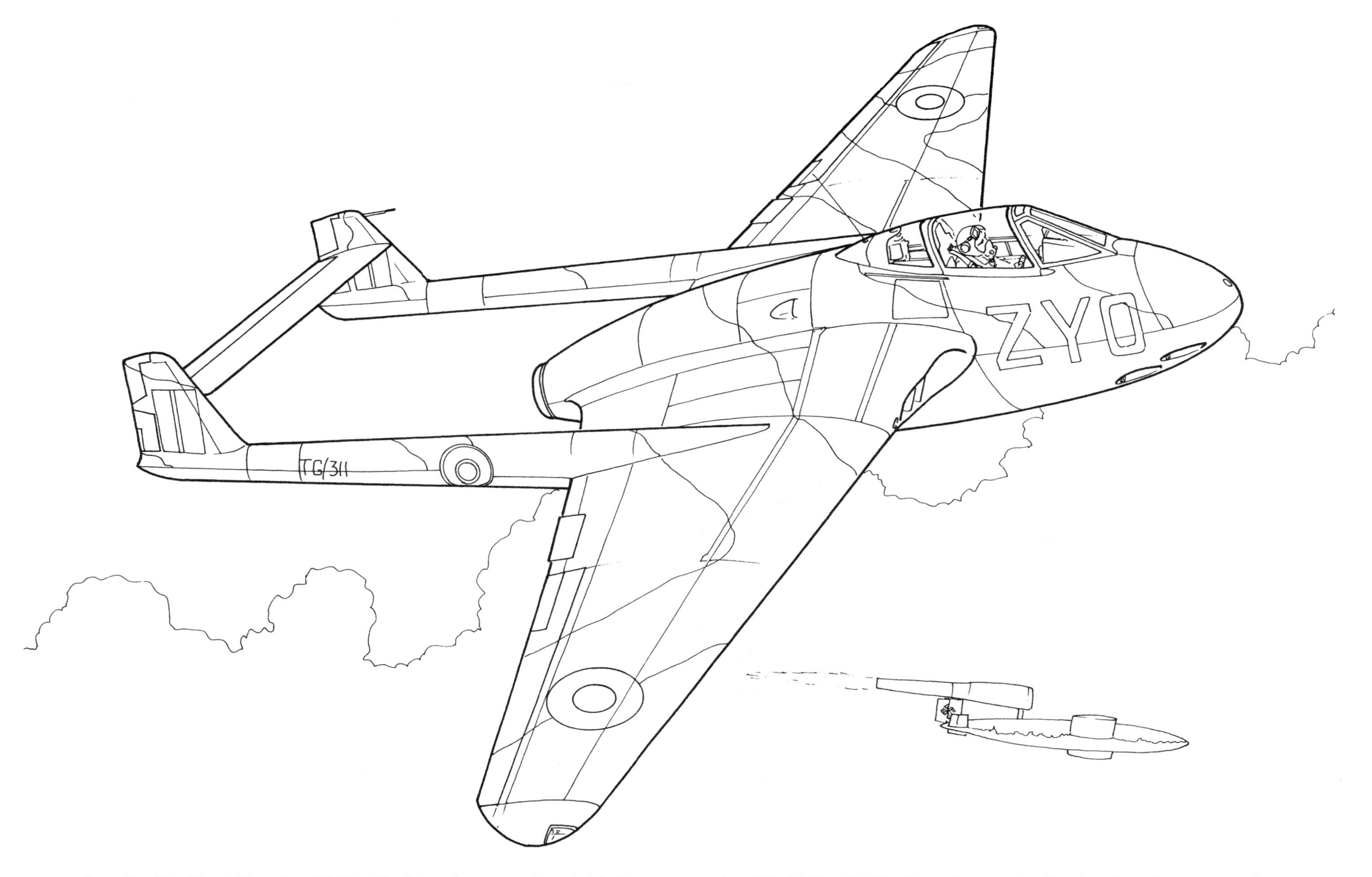

5. De Havilland Vampire (1943). The Vampire was a Royal Air Force fighter that could fly up to 500 mph. Although it first flew in September 1943, production of the plane on a grand scale was not achieved until after World War II. The Vampire was the first jet aircraft to operate from a carrier at sea. It crossed the Atlantic for the first time in 1948.

6. Hawker Hunter 1 of 43 Sqdn. A single-seater fighter-interceptor, the Hawker Hunter was developed.from the British World War II plane, the Hawker Hurricane. The first transonic British aircraft, the Hunter was first flown in 1953. A succession of improved production models appeared, with internal wing fuel and provision for drop tanks. This fighter was exported to Sweden, Denmark, and Peru. When production of the Hunter ended in 1959, a total of 1,972 had been built. Its maximum speed was 623 mph at 36,000 feet.

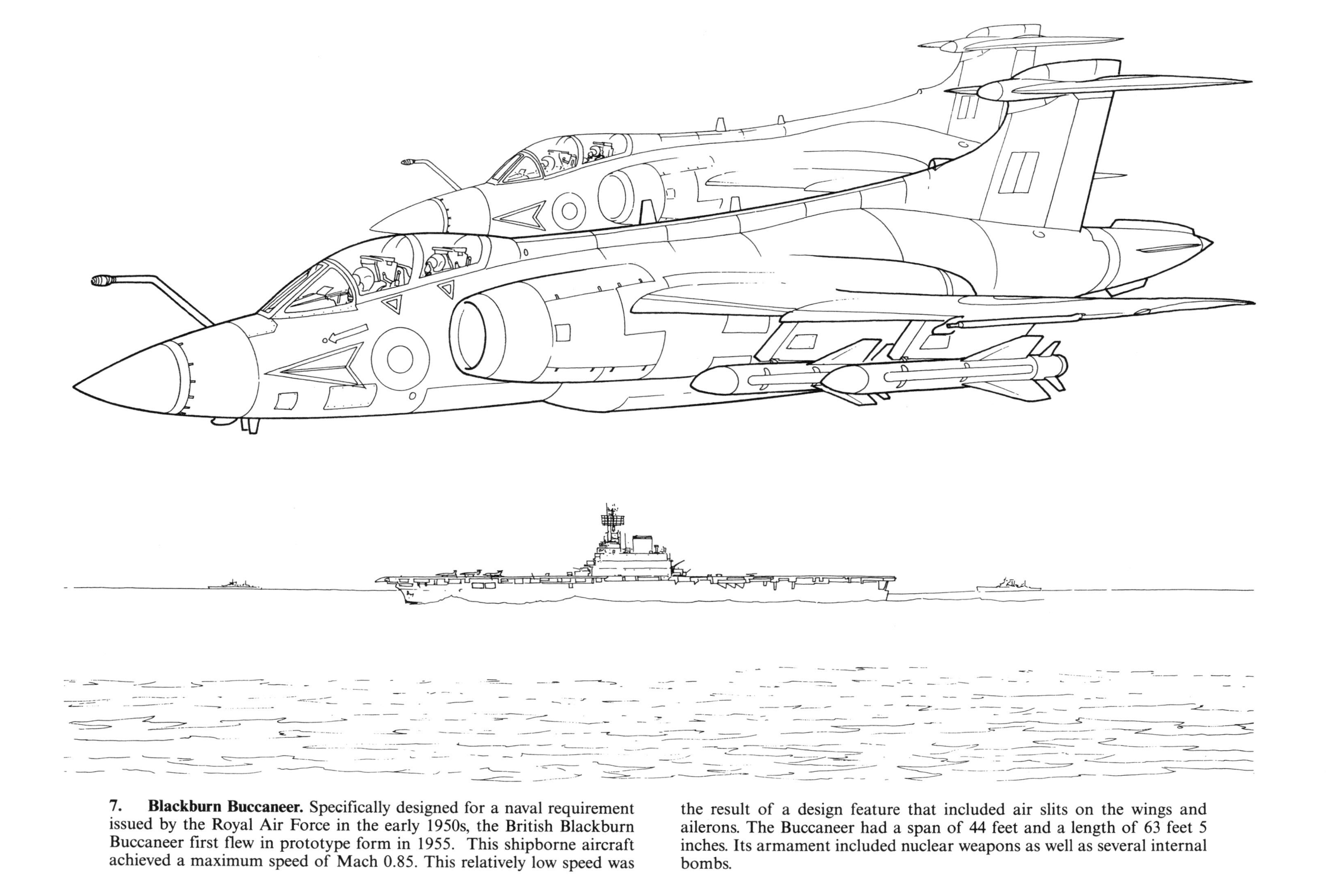

7. Blackburn Buccaneer. Specifically designed for a naval requirement issued by the Royal Air Force in the early 1950s, the British Blackburn Buccaneer first flew in prototype form in 1955. This shipborne aircraft achieved a maximum speed of Mach 0.85. This relatively low speed was the result of a design feature that included air slits on the wings and ailerons. The Buccaneer had a span of 44 feet and a length of 63 feet 5 inches. Its armament included nuclear weapons as well as several internal bombs.

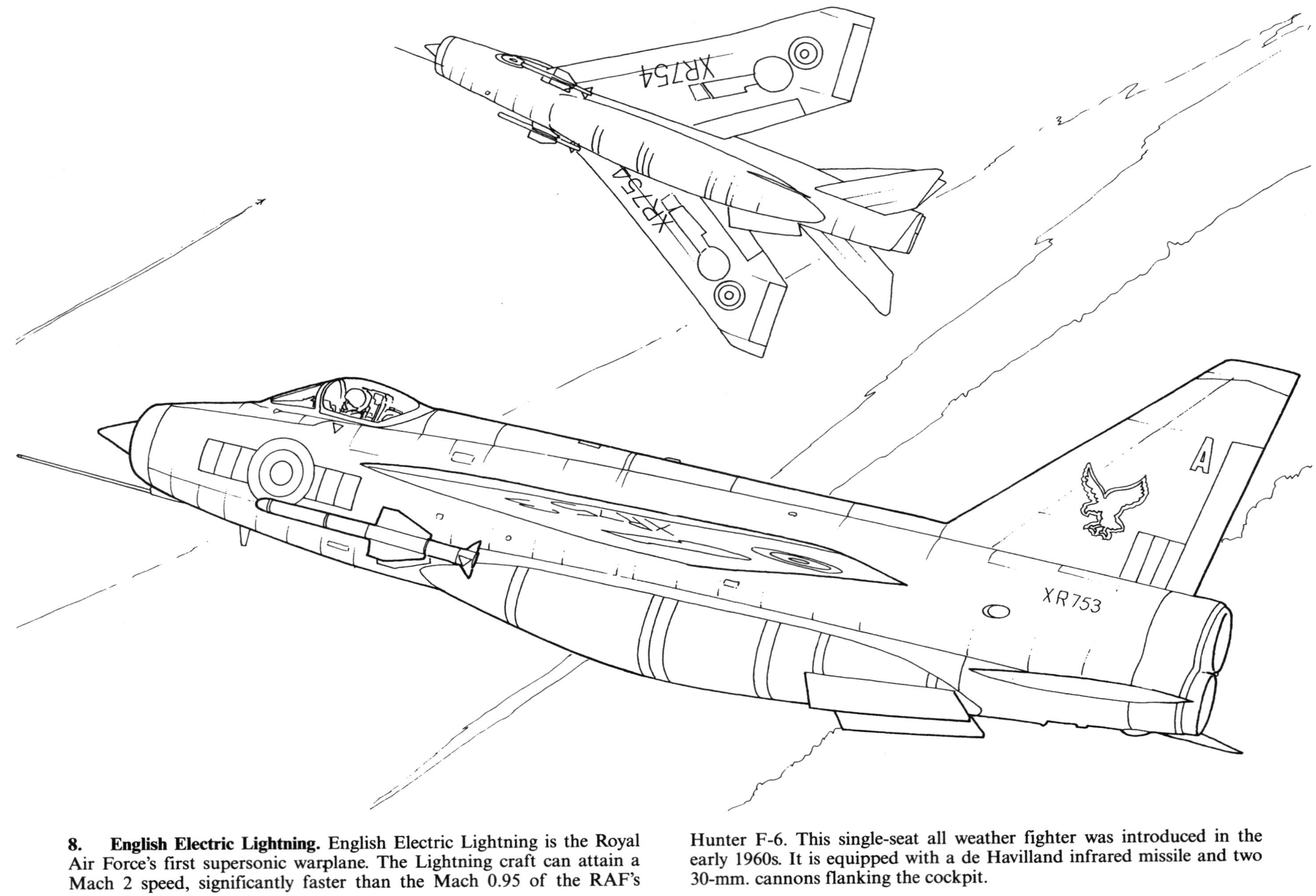

8. English Electric Lightning. English Electric Lightning is the Royal Air Force's first supersonic warplane. The Lightning craft can attain a Mach 2 speed, significantly faster than the Mach 0.95 of the RAF's Hunter F-6. This single-seat all weather fighter was introduced in the early 1960s. It is equipped with a de Havilland infrared missile and two 30-mm. cannons flanking the cockpit.

9. British Aerospace Harrier GR Mk 3. A close support and reconnaissance fighter, the British Aerospace Harrier was the world's first operational fixed-wing V/STOL (Vertical/Short Take-Off and Landing) combat aircraft. This means that the Harrier could take off straight up in the air without needing a runway. The Harrier GR Mk 1 first flew in 1967, but was soon upgraded to the GR Mk 3 (shown above). The Harrier flew at 720 mph at 1,000 feet. It was 45 feet 7¾ inches long and had a wingspan of 25 feet 3 inches.

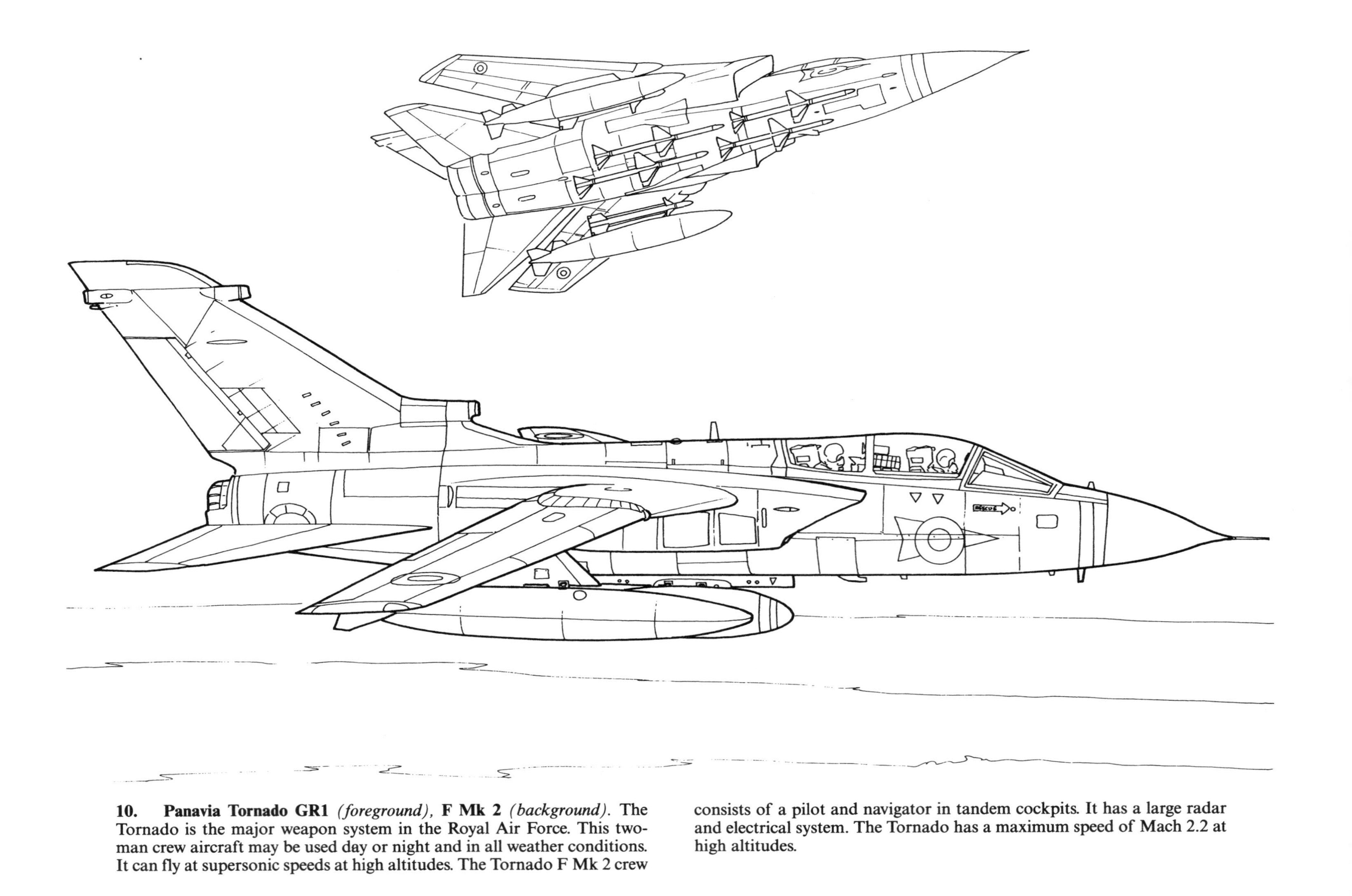

10. Panavia Tornado GR1 *(foreground)*, **F Mk 2** *(background)*. The Tornado is the major weapon system in the Royal Air Force. This two-man crew aircraft may be used day or night and in all weather conditions. It can fly at supersonic speeds at high altitudes. The Tornado F Mk 2 crew consists of a pilot and navigator in tandem cockpits. It has a large radar and electrical system. The Tornado has a maximum speed of Mach 2.2 at high altitudes.

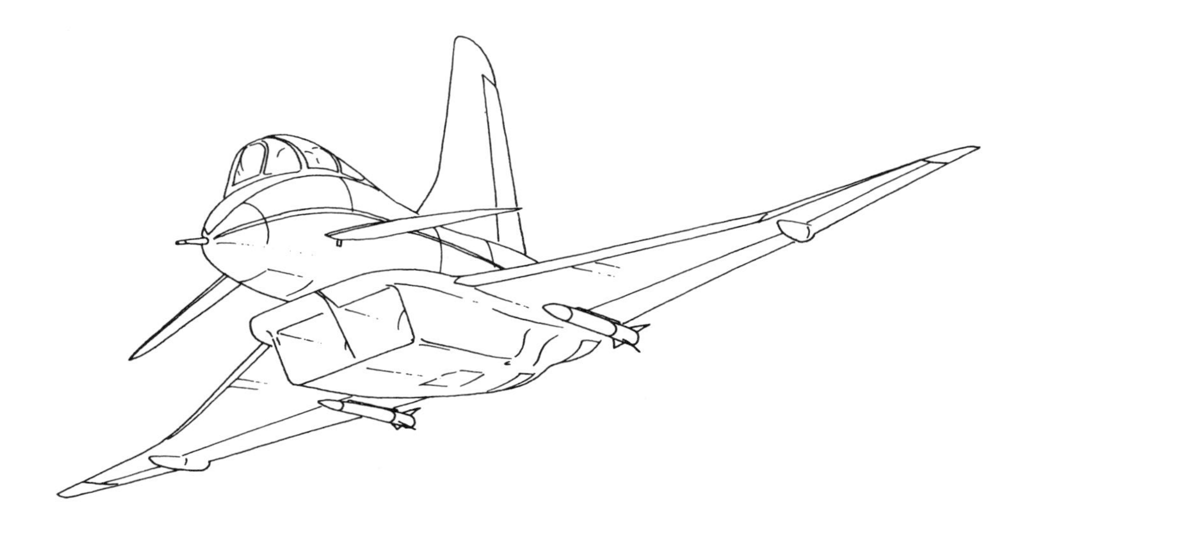

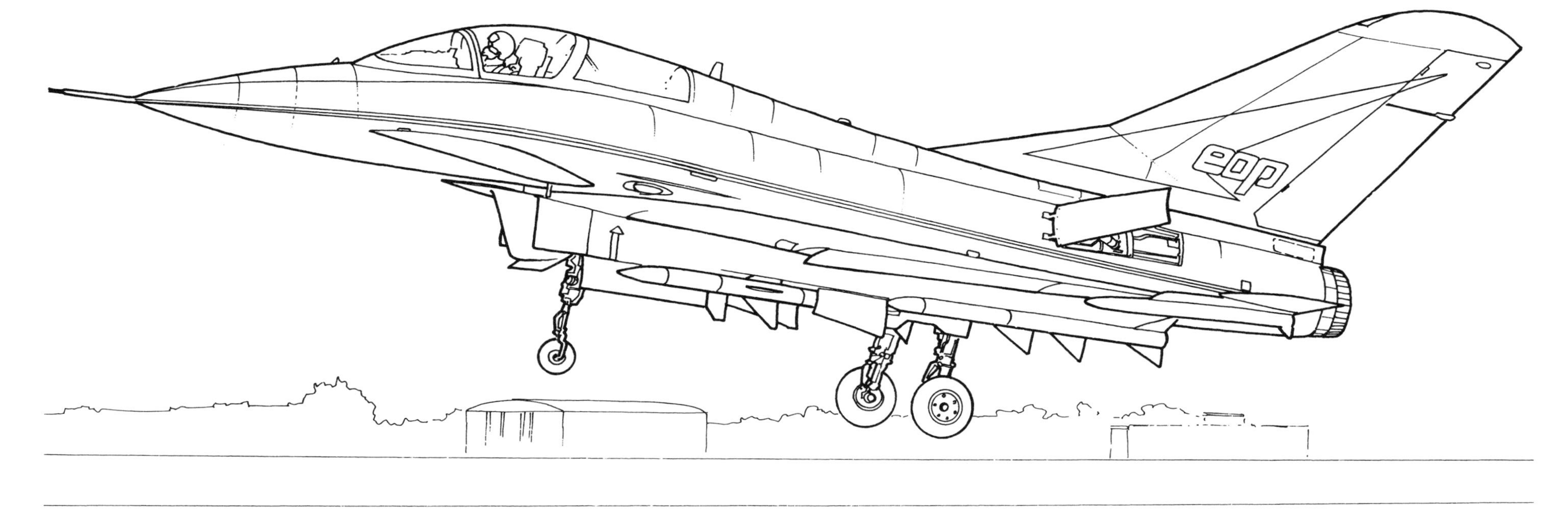

11. European Fighter Aircraft (EFA). Plans for the design of this aircraft, completed in 1992, go back over twenty years. The Royal Air Force wanted a ground attack craft, combining elements of the Jaguar and the Harrier. The EFA is a single-seat twin-engine jet fighter with a Mach 2 speed. It is 47 feet 6 inches long with a wingspan of 34 feet 5 inches.

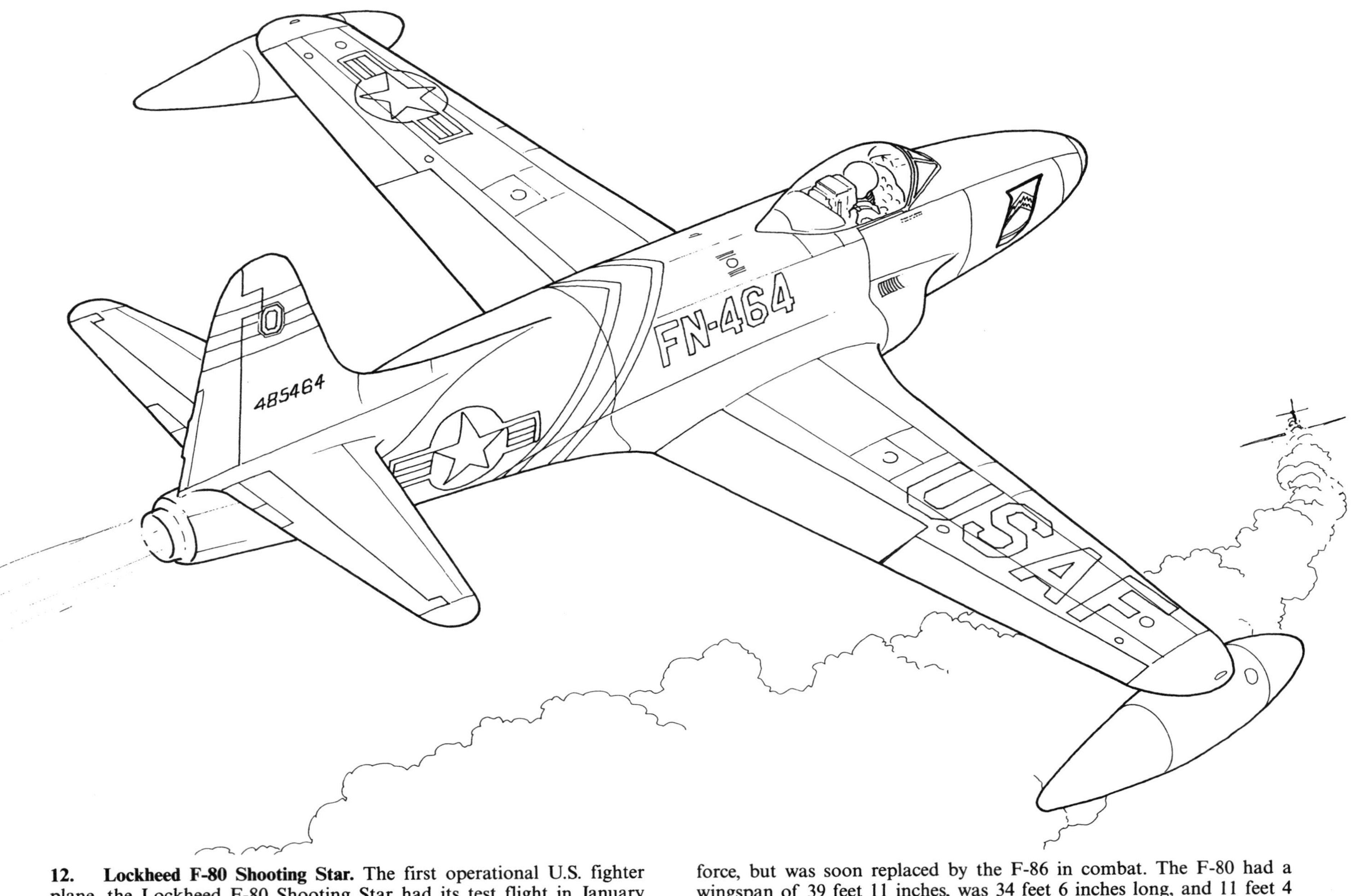

12. Lockheed F-80 Shooting Star. The first operational U.S. fighter plane, the Lockheed F-80 Shooting Star had its test flight in January 1944. This was the first jet fighter to join the U.S. Air Force and the first aircraft involved in jet-against-jet combat in 1950 during the Korean War. The F-80 fought against the Russian-built MiG-15 of the Chinese air force, but was soon replaced by the F-86 in combat. The F-80 had a wingspan of 39 feet 11 inches, was 34 feet 6 inches long, and 11 feet 4 inches tall. The Shooting Star set a new speed record, flying from the West coast to the East coast in 4 hours and 13 minutes.

13. Grumman F9F Cougar. A sweptwing variation of the Panther, the Cougar entered U.S. Navy service in 1952. Its span was 34 feet 6 inches, was 41 feet 9 inches long, and 12 feet 3 inches in height. During the Korean War, the Grumman F9F shot down several Russian MiG-15 fighters.

14. Chance Vought F7U-3 Cutlass. This carrier-based fighter contained heavier armament and had a greater range than its predecessor, the F7U-1. It first flew in prototype form in 1948 and had a unique structure for a combat aircraft. Its wingspan measured 39 feet 8 inches in length and it was 43 feet 1 inch long. Armament included four 20-mm. cannons plus 2,000 lbs. of bombs or rocket pods under the wings. The Cutlass, the first fighter designed to use afterburning for added thrust, was also the first aircraft to release bombs at supersonic speeds.

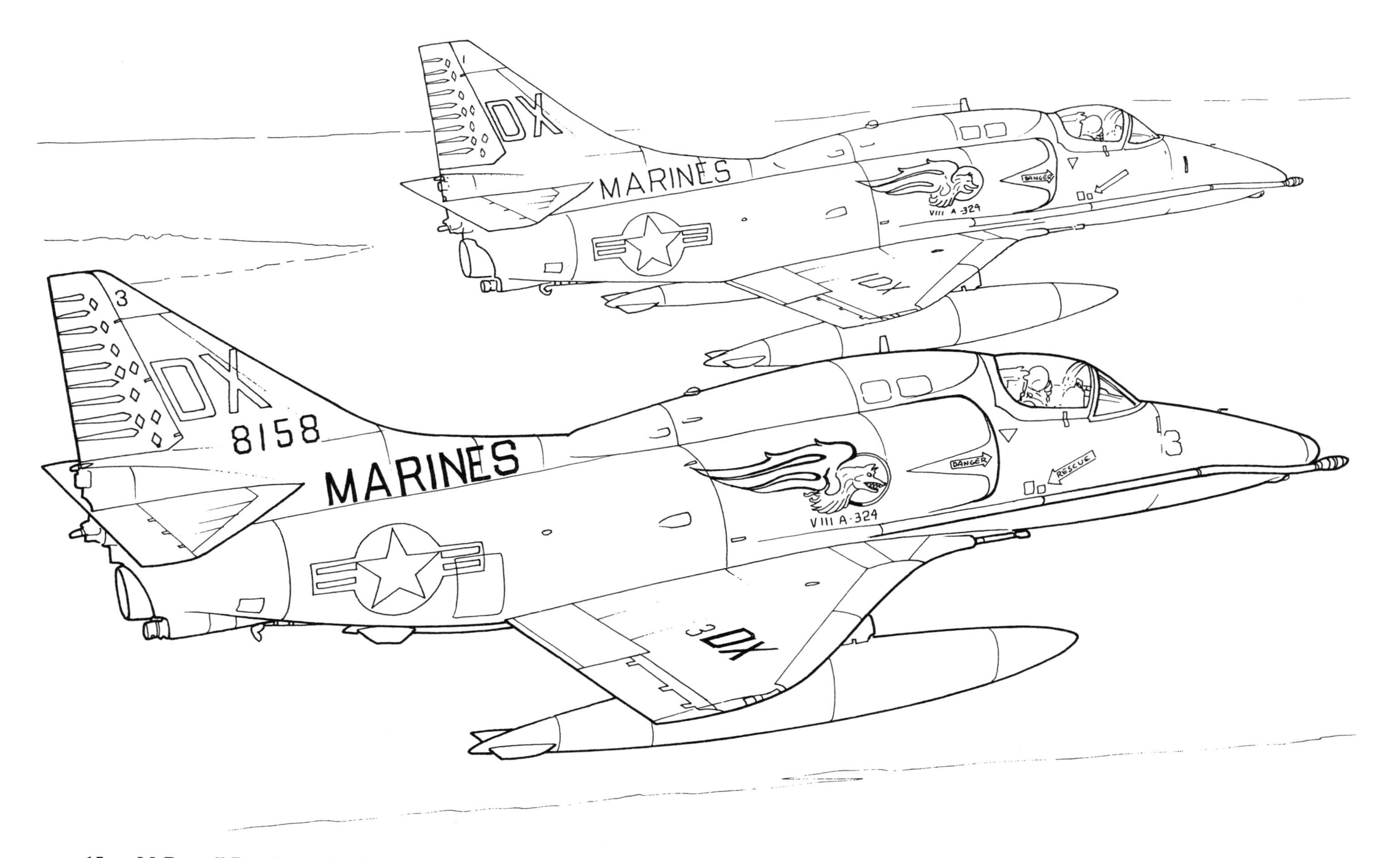

15. McDonnell Douglas A-4M Skyhawk. The Skyhawk has one of the longest unbroken production runs of any aircraft. The design of the Skyhawk was completed in 1952, and the aircraft had a successful operational record for over fifteen years. In addition to its use in the U.S. Navy and Marine Corps., the plane has also been deployed in Vietnam and Israel. The A-4M has five underwing stores stations and two built-in Mk 12 20-mm. guns.

16. Republic F-84 Thunderstreak. The F-84 Thunderstreak made its first flight in 1946 and many of these jet fighters were supplied to Allied nations. It became the first U.S. Air Force jet to carry a tactical atomic weapon. Attacks by the F-84 in Korea caused destructive flooding, which led to negotiations that saw the end of the Korean War on July 27, 1953. The Thunderstreak could carry six .50-caliber machine guns and eight 5-inch rockets or 2,000 lbs. of bombs or napalm tanks.

17. North American F-86F. This variant of the Sabre was created to counter the Russian-built MiG-15 during the Korean War. With swept-back wing and tail surfaces, the F-86F could fly up to 688 mph. It was 37 feet 1 inch long and 14 feet 9 inches high. Its armored cockpit and back-up systems ensured its safety in combat, but the added weight of these features contributed to its slower rate of climb, in comparison to the MiG-15. A more powerful engine was added, enabling the F-86F to achieve a rate of climb of 9,300 feet per minute. In addition, the F-86F was able to carry six .50-caliber machine guns.

18. McDonnell F-101H. Called the Voodoo, the F-101H bomber was initially designed as an escort fighter. However, the Voodoo was soon used for such tasks as interception, tactical/nuclear strike, and tactical reconnaissance. This versatile fighter, first flown in 1954, had a successful run with the U.S. Air Force for many years. It could reach a speed of Mach 1.51 and carried four cannons in the forward fuselage. This single seater was 69 feet 5 inches long and had a span of 39 feet 8 inches. Later versions of the Voodoo included the F-101B, which was a two-seater utilizing missile and rocket armament.

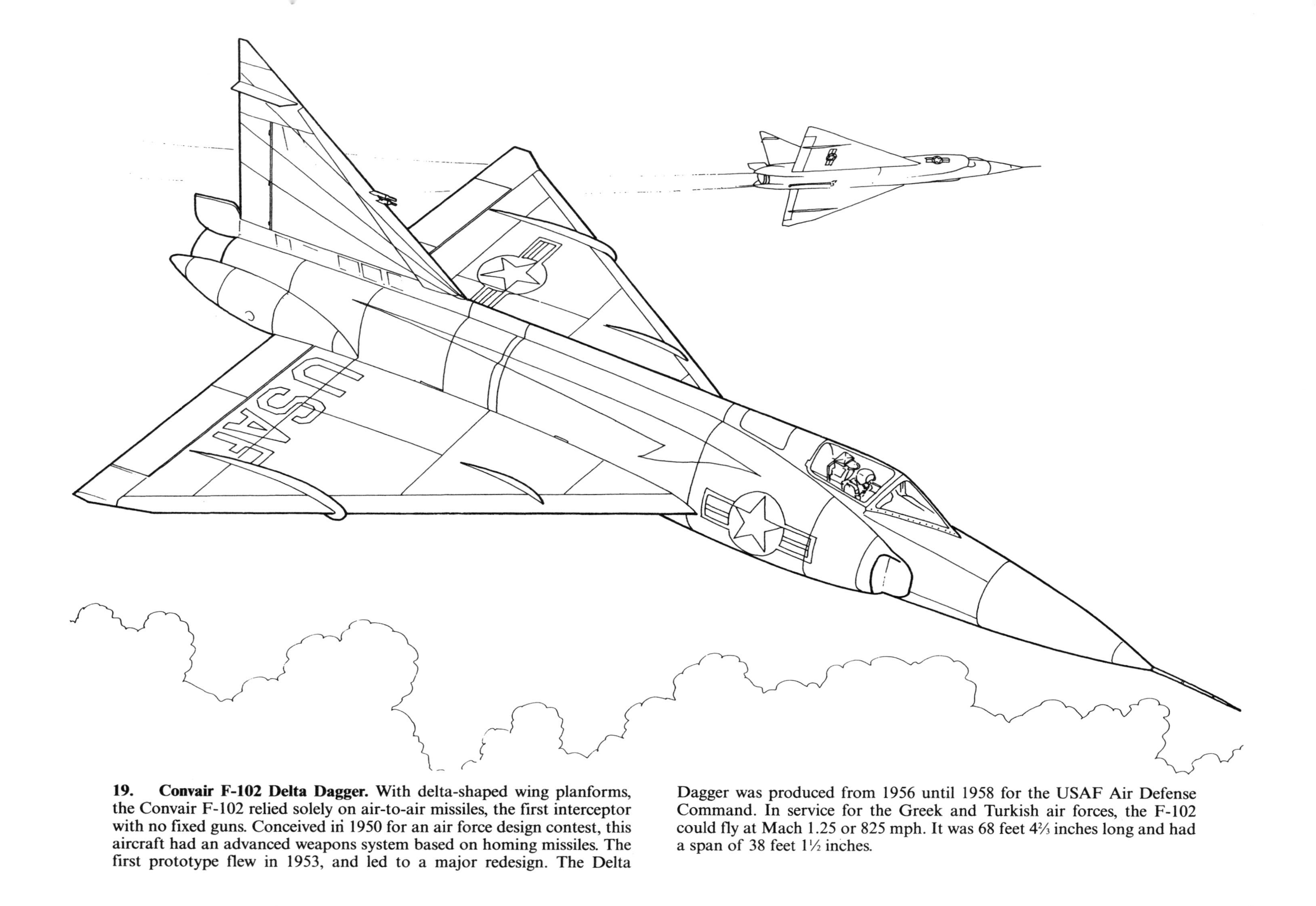

19. Convair F-102 Delta Dagger. With delta-shaped wing planforms, the Convair F-102 relied solely on air-to-air missiles, the first interceptor with no fixed guns. Conceived in 1950 for an air force design contest, this aircraft had an advanced weapons system based on homing missiles. The first prototype flew in 1953, and led to a major redesign. The Delta Dagger was produced from 1956 until 1958 for the USAF Air Defense Command. In service for the Greek and Turkish air forces, the F-102 could fly at Mach 1.25 or 825 mph. It was 68 feet 4⅔ inches long and had a span of 38 feet 1½ inches.

20. Lockheed F-104A and C Starfighter. The first aircraft to hold both world speed and altitude records at the same time, the F-104A Starfighter was accepted by the United States Air Force in 1958. The design of this fighter plane was based on detailed flight data from such research aircraft as the Douglas X-4. The F-104A was succeeded by the F-104C, which was 54 feet 8 inches long, had a wingspan of 21 feet 9 inches, and could climb 54,000 feet per minute. It set a speed record of 1,404 mph in 1958. The Starfighter was capable of flying supersonic straight up and was also the first fighter to carry a Vulcan 20-mm. revolving cannon.

21. Republic F-105D Thunderchief. The Republic F-105D could fly into combat with an astounding array of 4,000 different types of weapons stores. A single-seat all-weather strike fighter, it used guns, rockets, bombs, and napalm. It was used heavily for bombing enemy targets in Vietnam. This radar-equipped bomber plane was designed to carry nuclear and highly explosive bombs. Its top speed was 1,372 mph, was 64 feet 5 inches in length, and its span was 34 feet 11 inches.

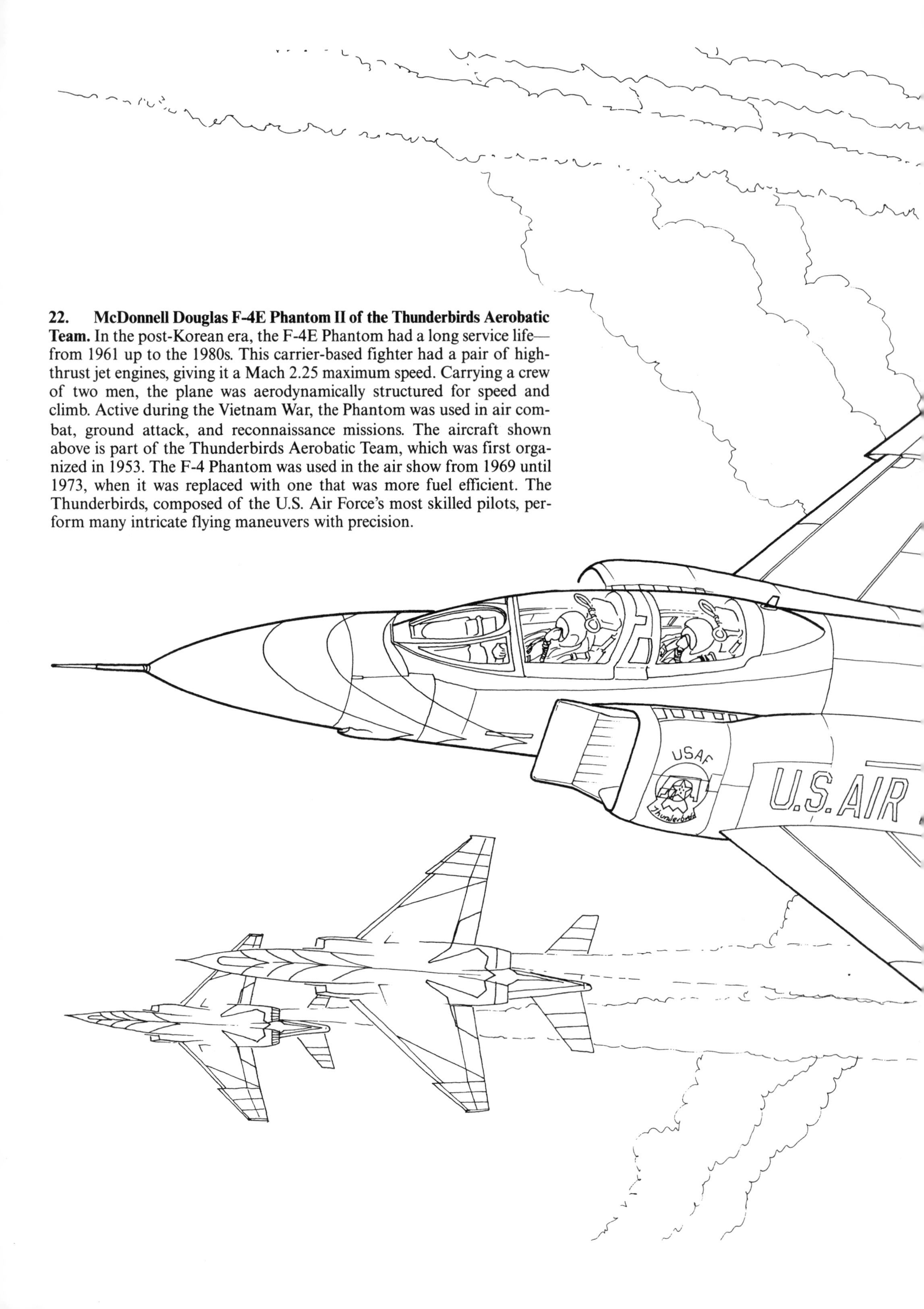

22. McDonnell Douglas F-4E Phantom II of the Thunderbirds Aerobatic Team. In the post-Korean era, the F-4E Phantom had a long service life—from 1961 up to the 1980s. This carrier-based fighter had a pair of high-thrust jet engines, giving it a Mach 2.25 maximum speed. Carrying a crew of two men, the plane was aerodynamically structured for speed and climb. Active during the Vietnam War, the Phantom was used in air combat, ground attack, and reconnaissance missions. The aircraft shown above is part of the Thunderbirds Aerobatic Team, which was first organized in 1953. The F-4 Phantom was used in the air show from 1969 until 1973, when it was replaced with one that was more fuel efficient. The Thunderbirds, composed of the U.S. Air Force's most skilled pilots, perform many intricate flying maneuvers with precision.

RCE

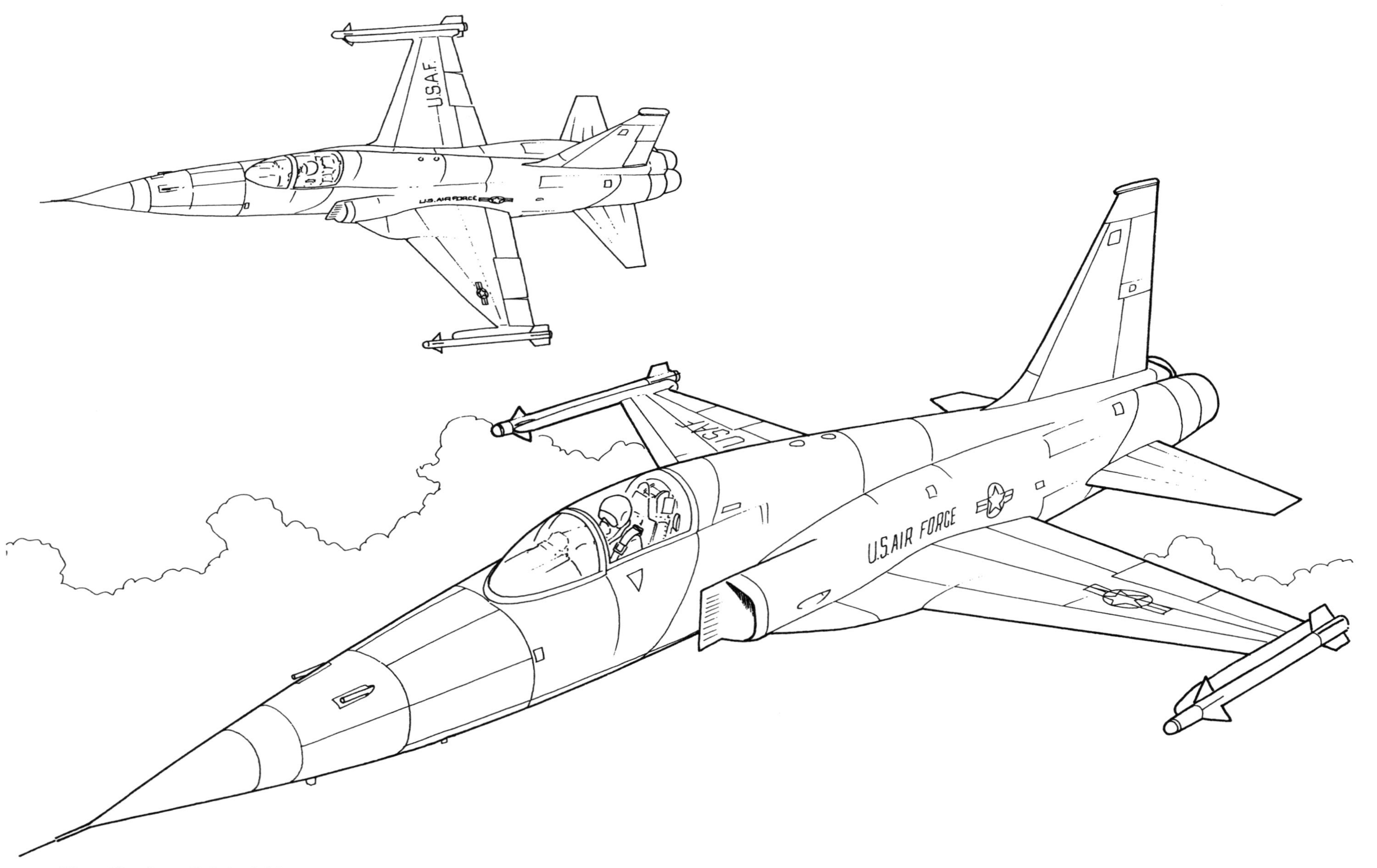

23. Northrop F-5. Weighing less than half of an F-4 Phantom, this single-seat supersonic fighter was developed in 1954. Its smaller design was intended to reduce the increasing size, weight, and cost of combat aircraft. The first F-5A was flown in 1963 and was used for short-range missions. Many foreign countries acquired this plane for their own air forces when production was completed in 1972. It was 47 feet 2 inches long and had a wingspan of 25 feet 3 inches.

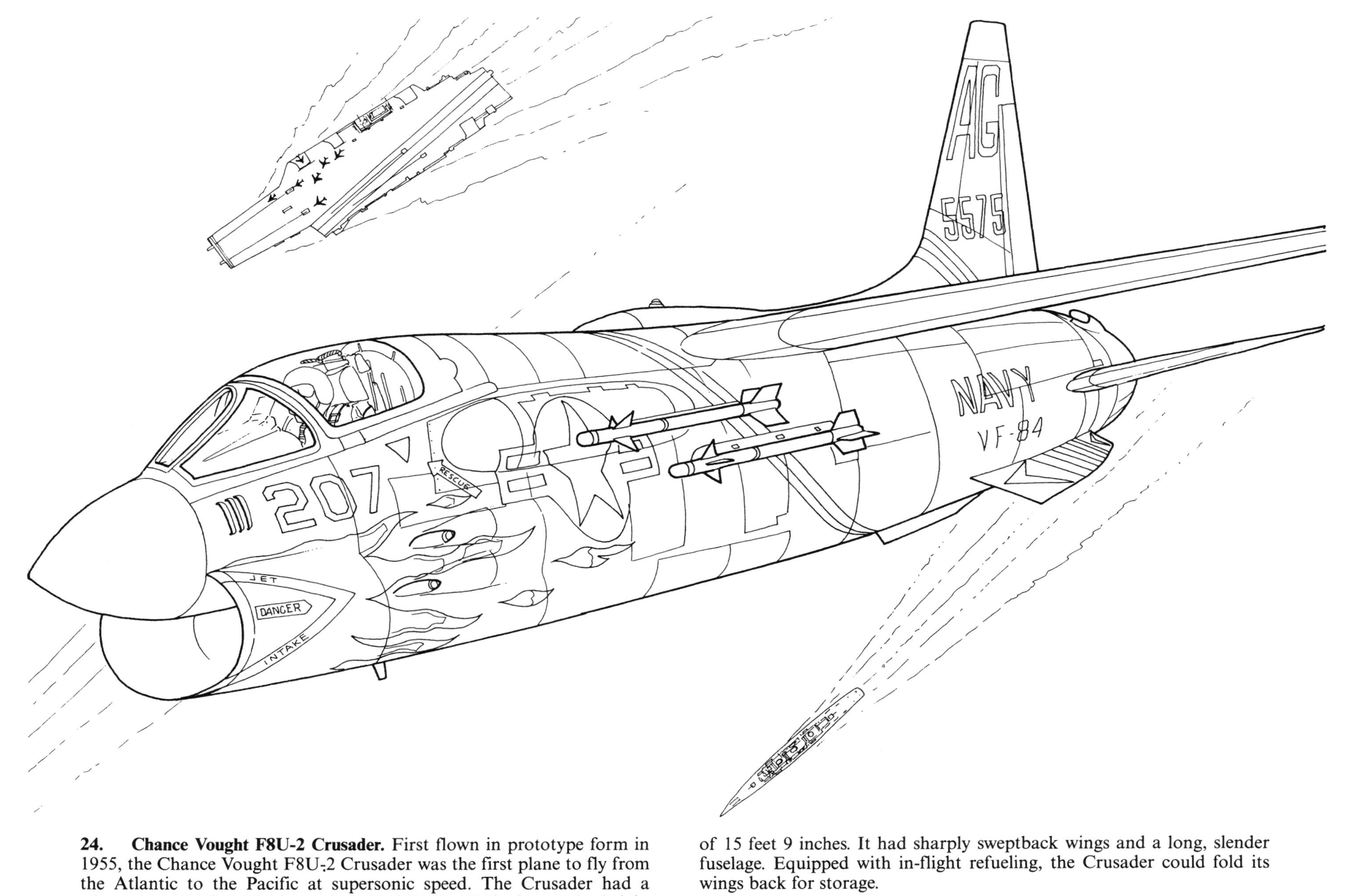

24. Chance Vought F8U-2 Crusader. First flown in prototype form in 1955, the Chance Vought F8U-2 Crusader was the first plane to fly from the Atlantic to the Pacific at supersonic speed. The Crusader had a wingspan of 35 feet 2 inches, a length of 54 feet 5¾ inches, and a height of 15 feet 9 inches. It had sharply sweptback wings and a long, slender fuselage. Equipped with in-flight refueling, the Crusader could fold its wings back for storage.

25. Grumman F-14A Tomcat. The Tomcat, designed for ground attack, for fleet defense, and as fighter escort, made its first flight in 1970. It had a two-man crew of pilot and weapons officer. The F-14A, powered by two Pratt & Whitney turbofans, housed a 20-mm. rotary cannon and up to ten missiles. Eighty F-14As were delivered to Iran in 1976–78. It could reach a speed of Mach 2.34, had a maximum span of 64 feet 1½ inches, and was nearly 62 feet long.

26. McDonnell Douglas F-15E. First flown in 1972, this single-seater aircraft could reach an incredible speed of Mach 2.5. Designed for air superiority, the F-15E contained a radar system that was able to detect small enemy fighters and rockets. Its armament consisted of a 20-mm. multibarrel cannon, four Sidewinder and four Sparrow missiles. In addition to air-to-air duties, the F-15E is also capable of long-range, day or night air-to-ground missions.

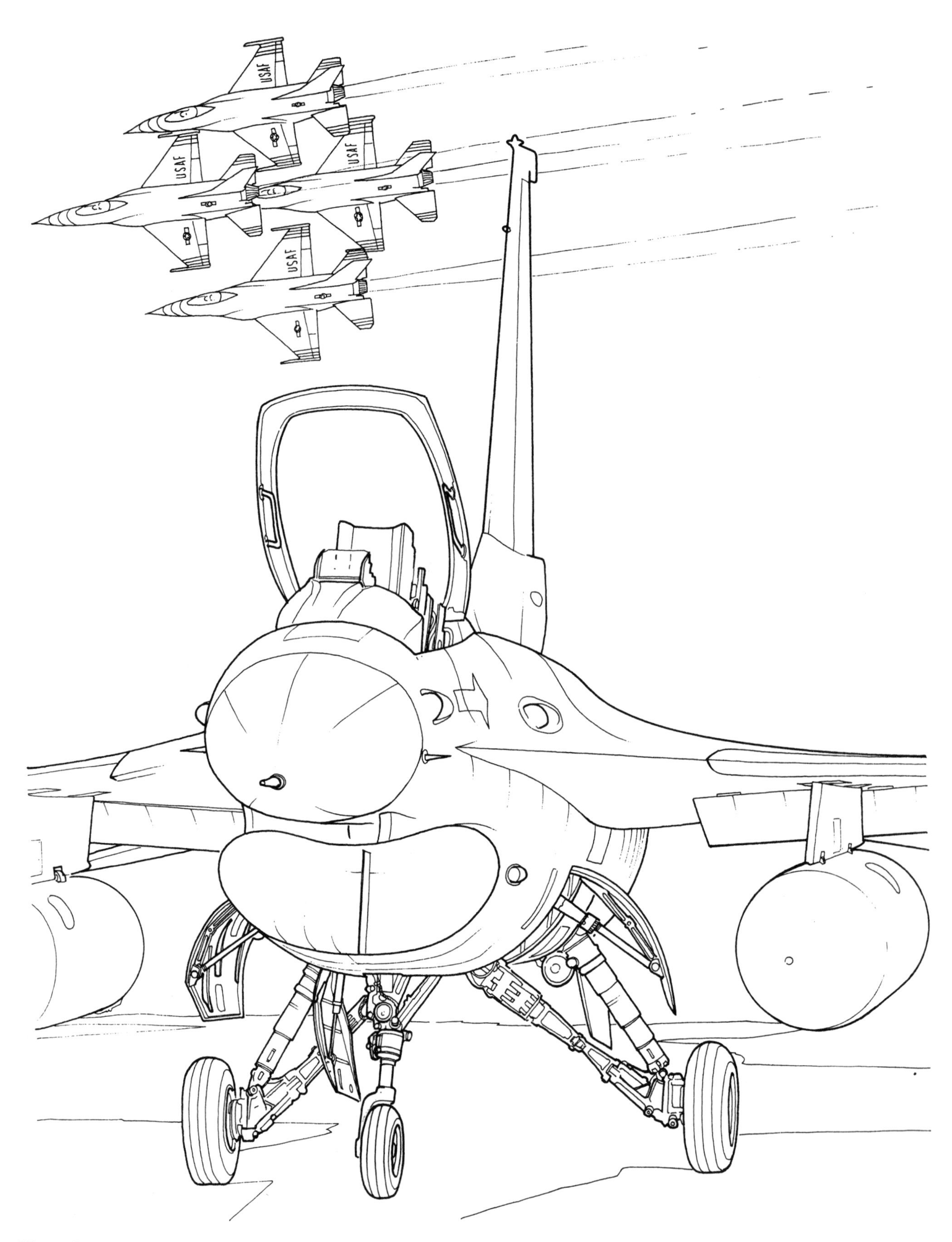

27. General Dynamics F-16. Sharing many of the same features as the McDonnell Douglas F-15E, the F-16 was smaller and lighter, with an engine that placed its speed within the Mach 2 range. A decrease in structural weight, a special canopy shape for high visibility, and a cockpit better designed for a pilot's handling of high g-forces (gravity) during combat comprise the technological advances newly developed in the F-16. First flown in 1976, this jet was selected by the U.S. Air Force to replace the F-4 Phantom II and was also chosen to equip fighter squadrons in several NATO countries. By the 1990s, sales of the F-16 were estimated to have reached $15 billion.

28. McDonnell Douglas F/A-18 Hornet. Serving the U.S. Navy and the U.S. Marine Corps., the F-18 is a twin-jet all-weather fighter and attack aircraft. The F-18 is capable of catapult launch and can reach a speed of Mach 1.8. At 56 feet long and with a wingspan of 40 feet 5 inches, the Hornet has nine weapons stations. This single-seater was first flown in 1978, but production did not expand until 1980. Armament for air-to-air missions includes one 20-mm. rotary cannon and four missiles.

29. Lockheed F-117A Stealth Fighter. The development of the Stealth Fighter was advanced by computerized flight controls. A radar absorbing material (RAM) covers the F-117A's aluminum frame. In addition, faceted panels also help the plane to fly undetected. Infrared turrets are used for night vision. Operational since 1983, the Stealth Fighter carries a 2,000 lb., low-level laser-guided bomb. Although the F-117A cannot fly at supersonic speeds, its groundbreaking contribution to military aviation is that it can bypass enemy radar detection.

30. Israel Aircraft Industries Kfir C-1. First flown in 1972, the prototype of the Kfir C-1 contained the same American turbojet engine as in the F-4 Phantom. The frame of the aircraft was modeled after the French Mirage 5, with several differences. The cockpit layout was revised and a new fuel and electrical system were installed. The Kfir C-1 entered service with the Israeli Air Force in 1975 and operated as both an air-superiority fighter and a ground-attack platform. It contained seven weapons stores stations under the fuselage and wings.

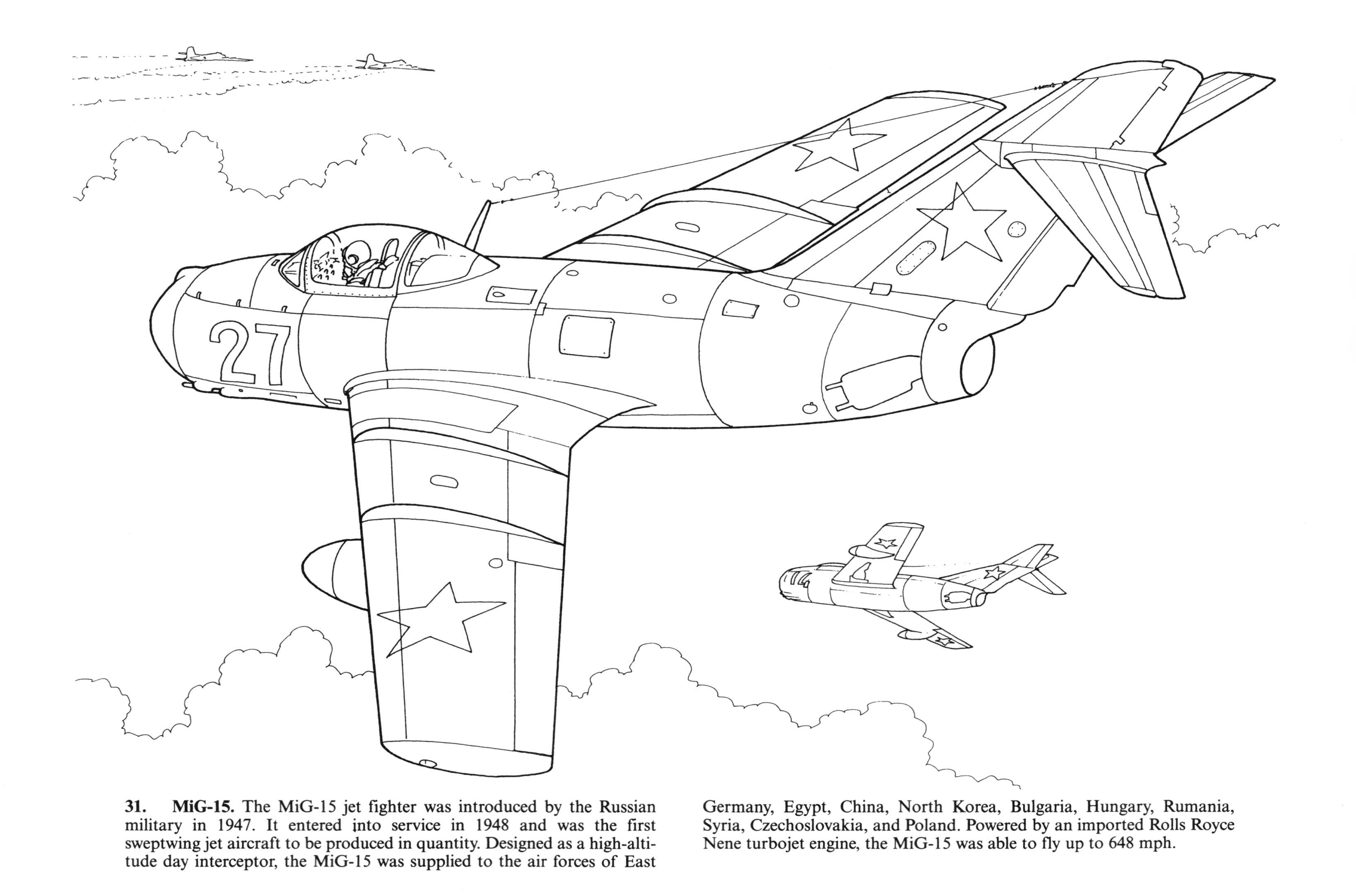

31. MiG-15. The MiG-15 jet fighter was introduced by the Russian military in 1947. It entered into service in 1948 and was the first sweptwing jet aircraft to be produced in quantity. Designed as a high-altitude day interceptor, the MiG-15 was supplied to the air forces of East Germany, Egypt, China, North Korea, Bulgaria, Hungary, Rumania, Syria, Czechoslovakia, and Poland. Powered by an imported Rolls Royce Nene turbojet engine, the MiG-15 was able to fly up to 648 mph.

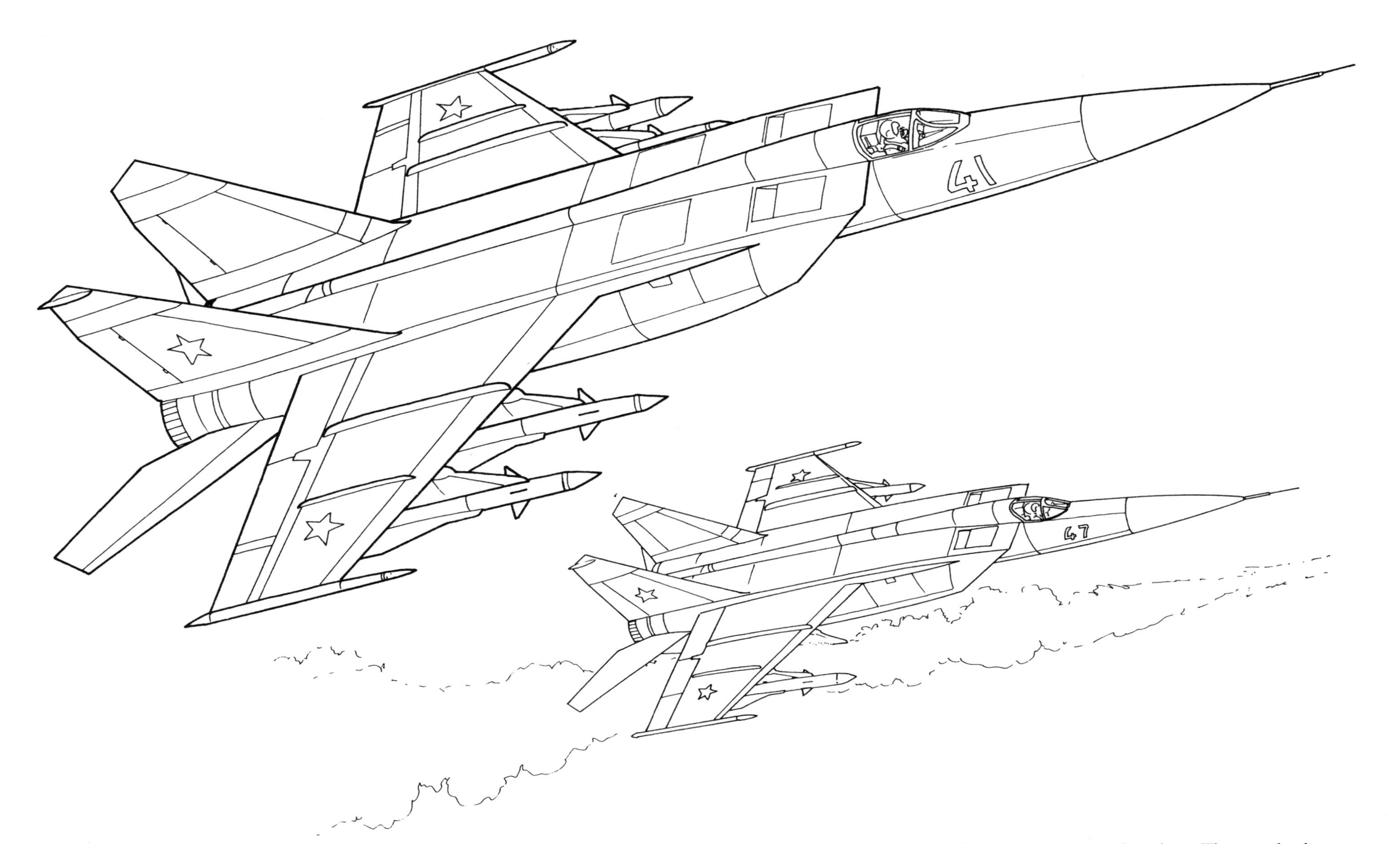

32. MiG-25 Foxbat. A Mikoyan-Gurevich high-altitude interceptor, the MiG-25 Foxbat first flew in prototype form in 1964. Made of steel, the MiG-25 was the fastest and highest flying combat aircraft of its time. From 1967–73, the Foxbat continued to set records for speed and altitude. Subsequent versions of the MiG-25 included reconnaissance versions, a two-seat training version, and one with upgraded engines. The standard MiG-25 had a maximum speed of 1,868 mph (Mach 3, nearly three times the speed of sound!) and a climb of 40,950 feet per minute. Production of this aircraft ceased in 1978.

33. MiG-21 MF (Fishbed-J). The MiG-21 air superiority fighter served as an all-weather interceptor. The MiG-21 MF first entered service in 1969 and differed from its predecessor, the MiG-21 PFMA, in one way: it added an R-13 engine. This fighter could fly at a speed of 1,385 mph, with a maximum climb of 21,000 feet per minute. Its span measured 23 feet 5½ inches and was 48 feet 7½ inches long.

34. MiG-23 K (Flogger F). First flown early in 1967, the MiG-23 featured a wing with three sweep settings. The MiG-23 K, introduced in 1971, was used in limited service. It was powered by a Lyulka engine and its armament included a twin-barrel 23-mm. cannon and up to four missiles.

35. MiG-29 Fulcrum. First operational in the Soviet Air Force in 1985, the MiG-29 is a single-seat counterair fighter. Exported to Syria and India after 1986, the MiG-29 was first flown as a prototype as early as 1976. The MiG-29, or Fulcrum, carries one 23-mm. or 30-mm. six-barrel cannon and up to six missiles. It also includes other equipment such as infrared search and tracking, Doppler radar for day and night all-weather capability, and a digital data link. The MiG-29 can reach a maximum speed of 1,518 mph.

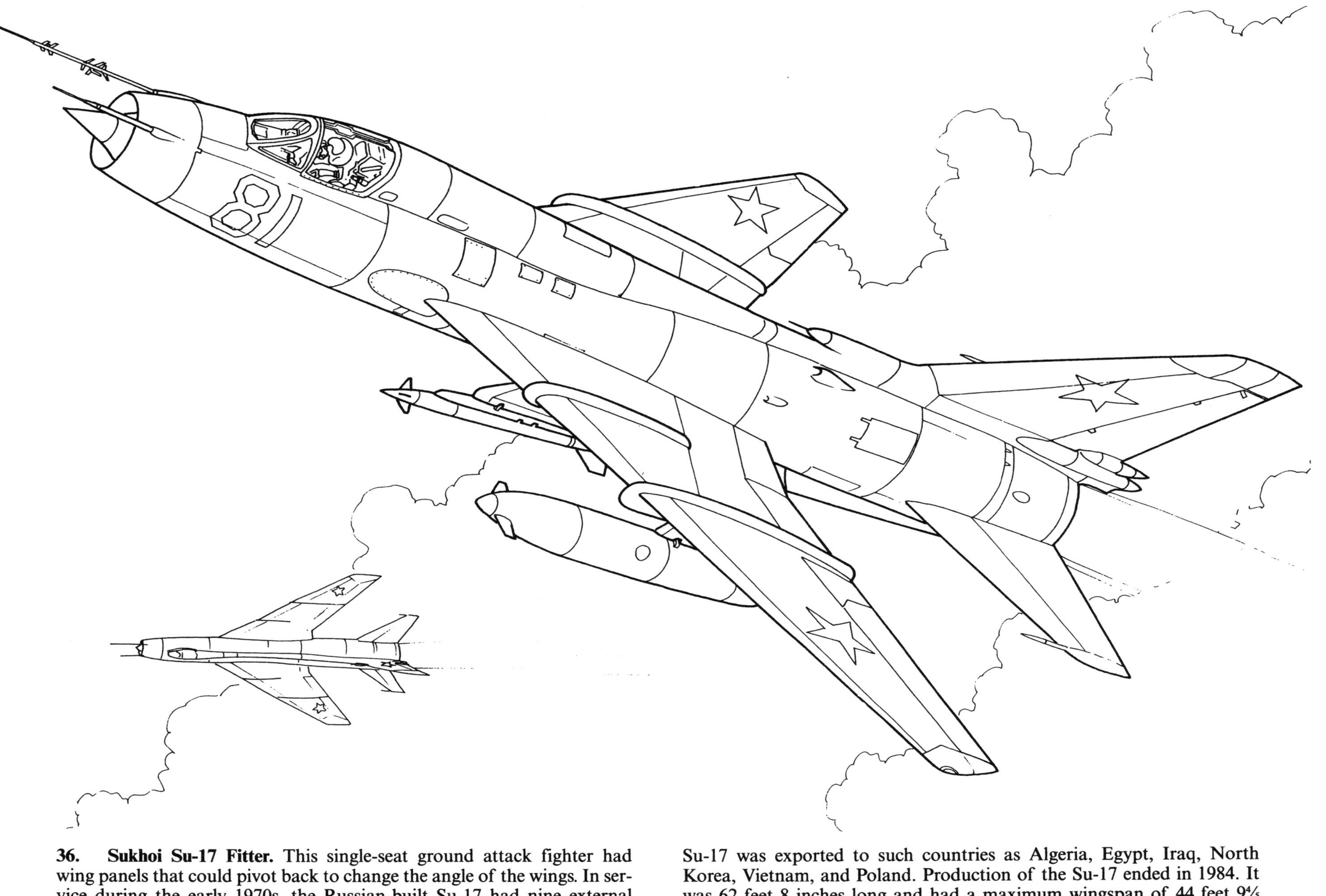

36. Sukhoi Su-17 Fitter. This single-seat ground attack fighter had wing panels that could pivot back to change the angle of the wings. In service during the early 1970s, the Russian-built Su-17 had nine external weapons stores and two built-in 30-mm. cannons. A newer version of the Su-17 was exported to such countries as Algeria, Egypt, Iraq, North Korea, Vietnam, and Poland. Production of the Su-17 ended in 1984. It was 62 feet 8 inches long and had a maximum wingspan of 44 feet 9⅘ inches.

37. Sukhoi Su-27. The prototype for the Su-27 was first flown in 1981. A tandem two-seat training version was flown in 1985. Able to achieve a maximum speed of Mach 2.35, the Russian Su-27 had an armament consisting of one 30-mm. cannon and radar-homing missiles located on the fuselage and wings. Twenty-four Su-27s were exported to China in 1992. With a wingspan reaching 48 feet 2¾ inches, this aircraft was nearly 72 feet in length.

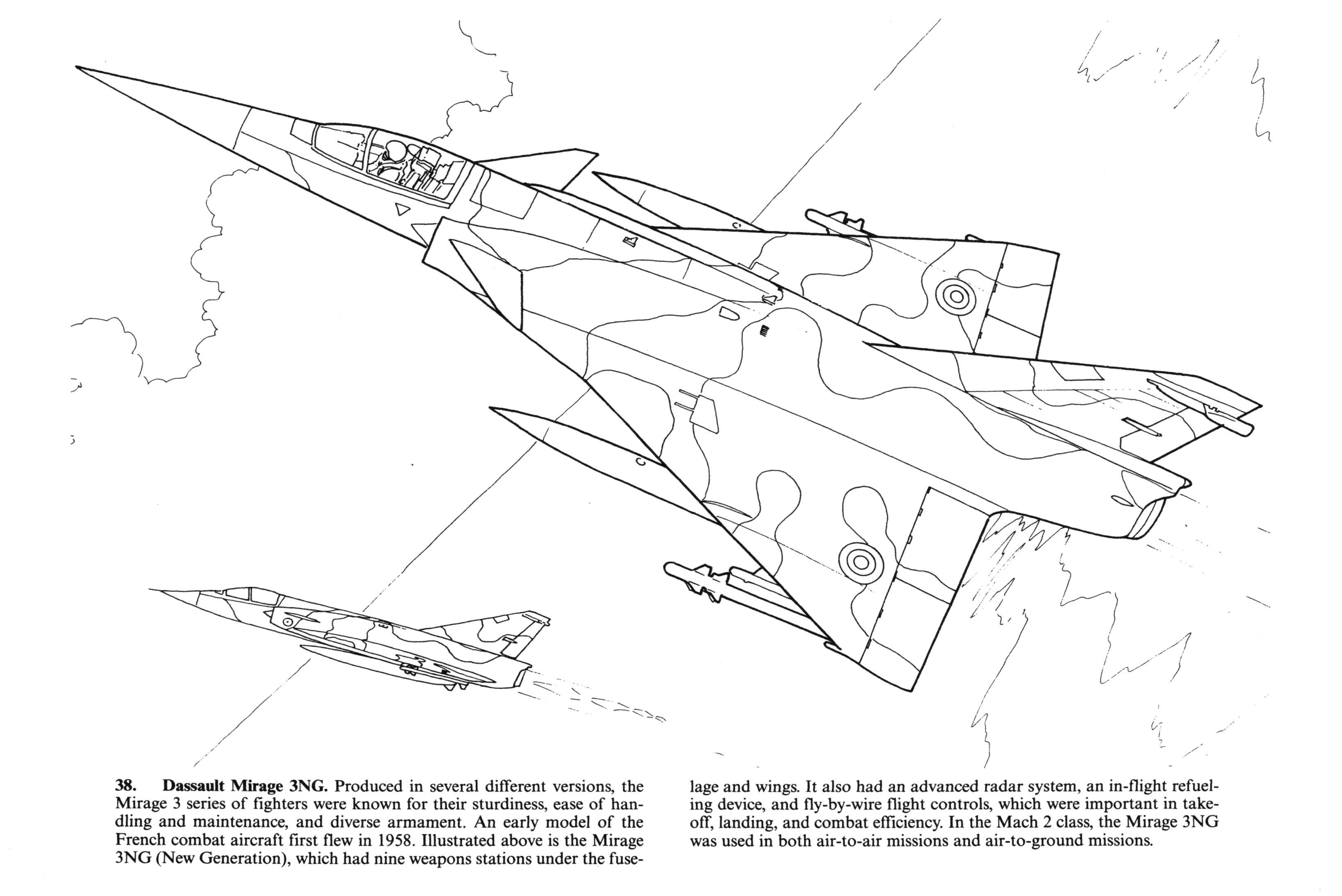

38. Dassault Mirage 3NG. Produced in several different versions, the Mirage 3 series of fighters were known for their sturdiness, ease of handling and maintenance, and diverse armament. An early model of the French combat aircraft first flew in 1958. Illustrated above is the Mirage 3NG (New Generation), which had nine weapons stations under the fuselage and wings. It also had an advanced radar system, an in-flight refueling device, and fly-by-wire flight controls, which were important in takeoff, landing, and combat efficiency. In the Mach 2 class, the Mirage 3NG was used in both air-to-air missions and air-to-ground missions.

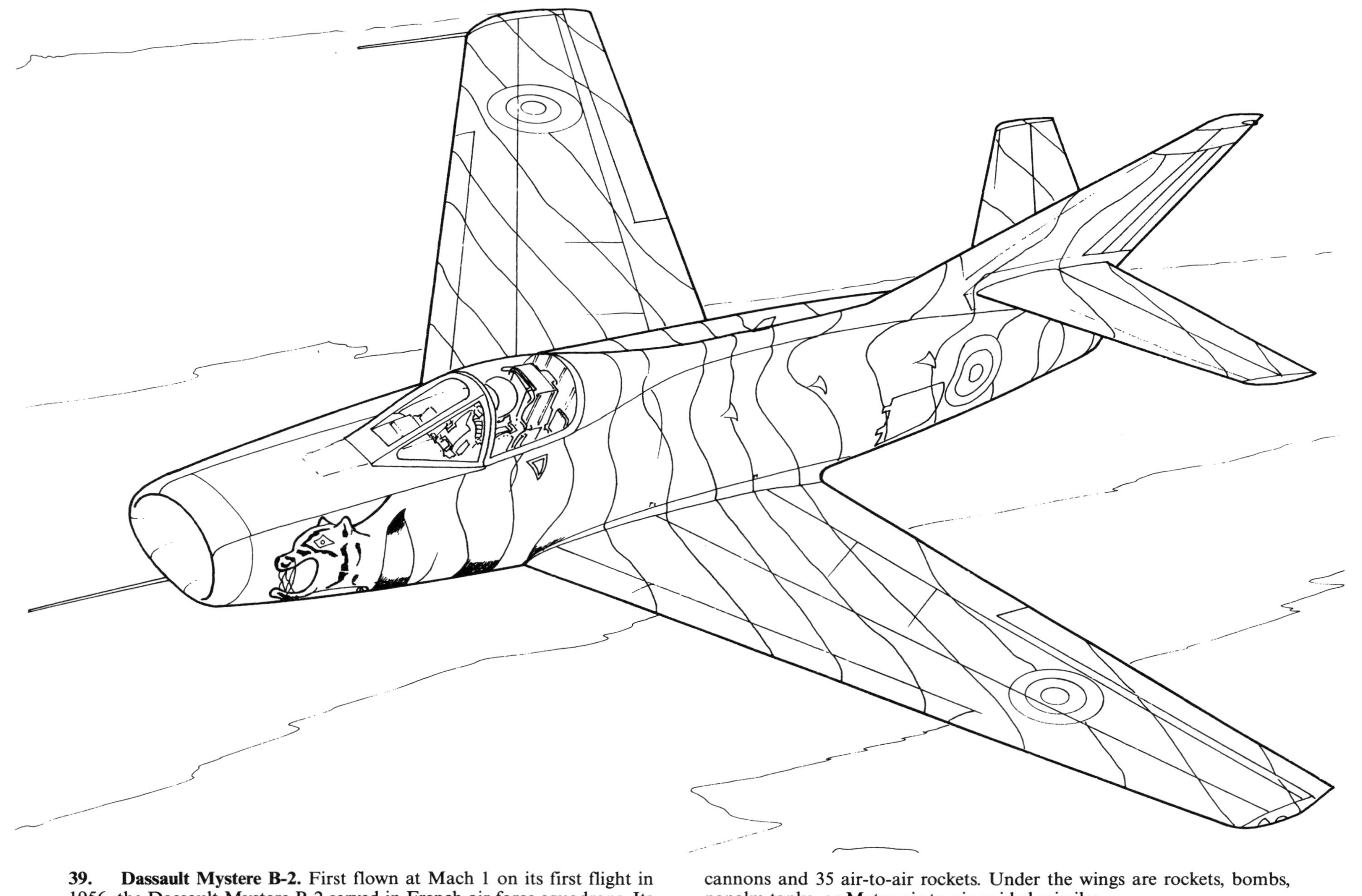

39. Dassault Mystere B-2. First flown at Mach 1 on its first flight in 1956, the Dassault Mystere B-2 served in French air force squadrons. Its rate of climb is 29,500 feet per minute. Its fuselage hides two 30-mm. cannons and 35 air-to-air rockets. Under the wings are rockets, bombs, napalm tanks, or Matra air-to-air guided missiles.

40. Dassault Rafale A. This single-seater supersonic aircraft is an experimental prototype. The design of the plane includes a twin-engine layout and a new aerodynamic planform. The Rafale is 51 feet 10 inches long with a wingspan of 36 feet 1 inch. It can attain a maximum speed in level flight of Mach 2.

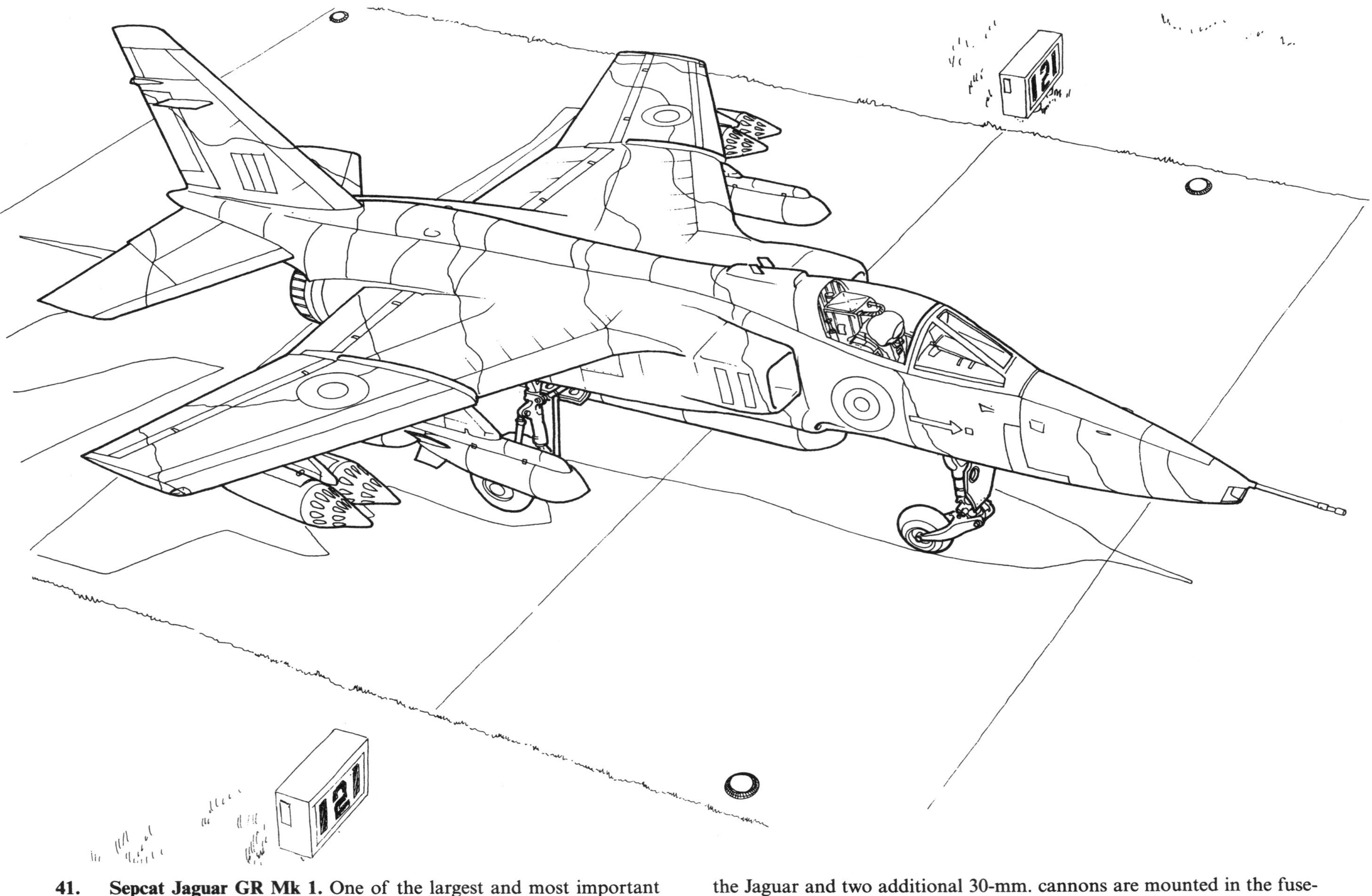

41. Sepcat Jaguar GR Mk 1. One of the largest and most important aircraft in production in Europe during the early 1970s, the Jaguar was first operational in 1973. When the first prototype flew in 1968, Britain and France ordered 400 planes. Five weapons stations can be carried on the Jaguar and two additional 30-mm. cannons are mounted in the fuselage. The large fuel capacity gives this aircraft an advantage, and it is able to attack at high speeds.

42. Fiat G. 91. This lightweight Italian fighter was used by NATO for tactical missions. It carried a mixed armament of rockets, machine guns, and guided missiles. It could reach a speed of Mach 0.91. The prototype first flown in 1956, the Fiat G. 91, was 34 feet 2½ inches in length with a span of 28 feet 1 inch. Other variants of the G. 91 included two-seat trainers and reconnaissance aircraft.

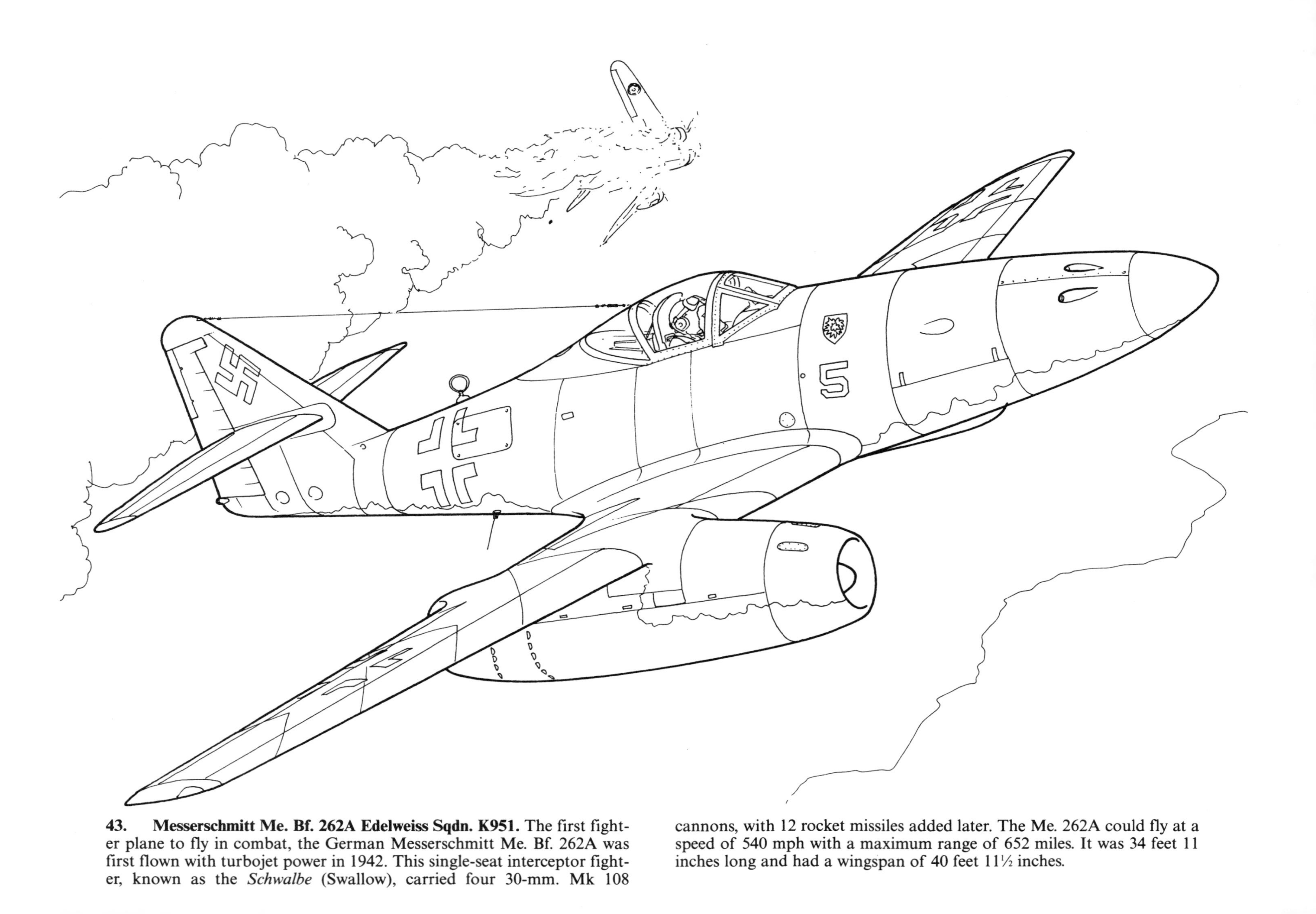

43. Messerschmitt Me. Bf. 262A Edelweiss Sqdn. K951. The first fighter plane to fly in combat, the German Messerschmitt Me. Bf. 262A was first flown with turbojet power in 1942. This single-seat interceptor fighter, known as the *Schwalbe* (Swallow), carried four 30-mm. Mk 108 cannons, with 12 rocket missiles added later. The Me. 262A could fly at a speed of 540 mph with a maximum range of 652 miles. It was 34 feet 11 inches long and had a wingspan of 40 feet 11½ inches.

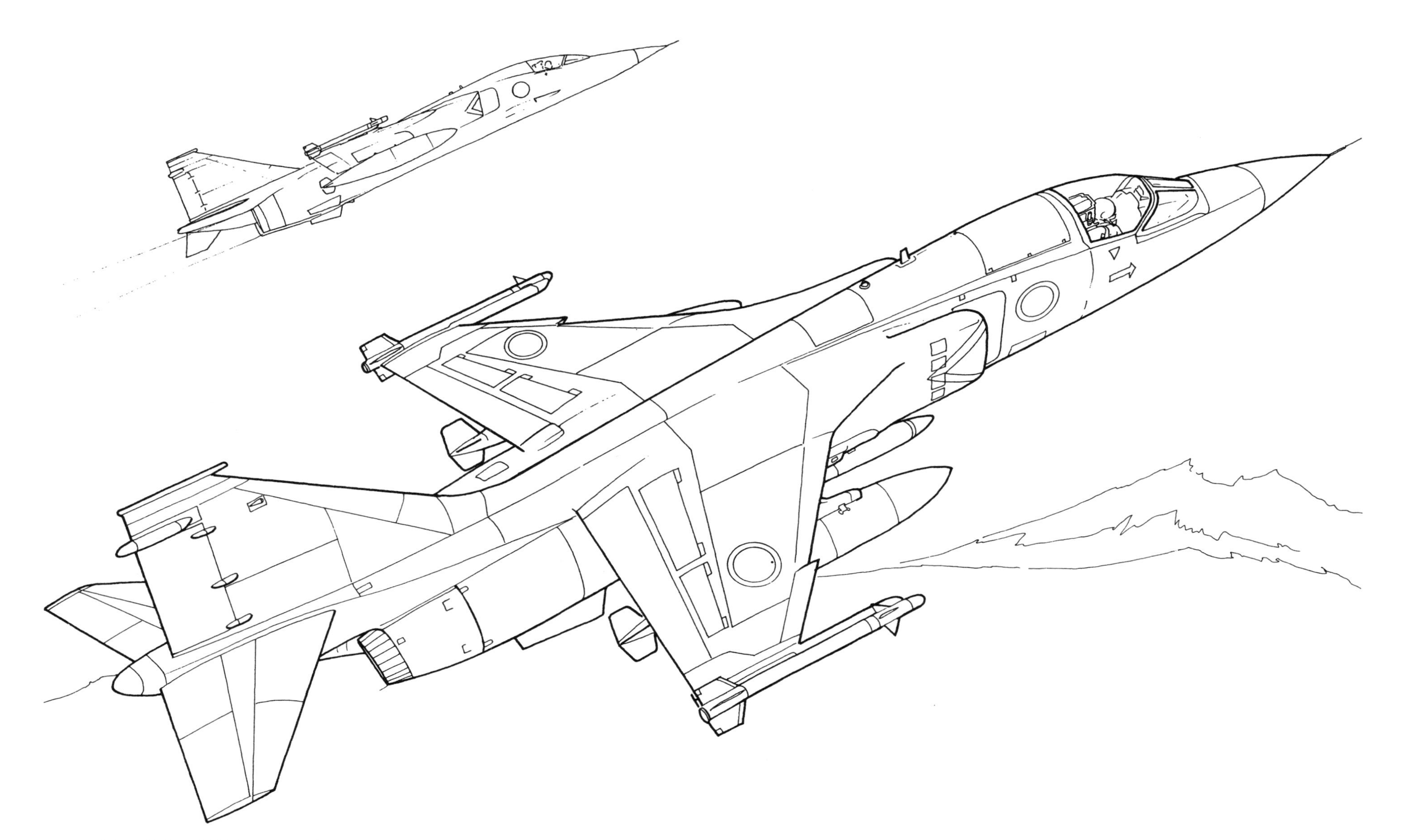

44. Mitsubishi F-1. Based on the Mitsubishi T-2 supersonic trainer, the Mitsubishi F-1 is a single-seat close air support fighter. This plane flew in prototype form in 1975. The F-1, the first Japanese-produced combat aircraft since the end of World War II, was armed with one 20-mm. cannon and could carry up to 6,000 lbs. of bombs or rockets on the fuselage and wings. Its wingspan was 25 feet 10¼ inches and it was 58 feet 7 inches in length.